Chess Versus Checkers

The Secret to Game-Changing Interviews

By Jack Ryan

Table of Contents

Chapter 1: The Hidden Language of the Interview............1

Chapter 2: Tell Me a Little Bit about Yourself....................10

Chapter 3: Good Times..27

Chapter 4: Bad Times..39

Chapter 5: Strengths...55

Chapter 6: Weaknesses...70

Chapter 7: Quick Hits..84

Chapter 8: Conclusion...101

Chapter 1:

The Hidden Language of the Interview

"So, Brent how did it go?" I inquired.

"I was playing chess, and they were playing checkers the whole interview. I have this job locked up."

This conversation is etched into my memory for two reasons. First, how could he be so confident he won the job? At least eight other applicants were interviewed for the same position that day. Brent was qualified for the position, but not uniquely so. Not to mention, there is no way he could know how the other candidates fared in their interviews. It is entirely possible other candidates had better resumes or shared more impressive accomplishments. Second, why use the, "checkers and chess" analogy? This seems counterintuitive. Don't you want to be on the same page as your interviewer? Shouldn't you answer the questions they ask as directly as possible? At least that's what we have always been taught... Right?

I soon realized both questions led to the same answer. The reason Brent could be so confident following his interview was precisely because he had not answered the questions he was **asked,** but instead listened to the question and **interpreted** which qualities the interviewer was hoping to identify in a potential future employee. Once he discovered what his interviewer was truly after, he told a story that highlighted how he possessed those exact qualities.

The truth is that in every interview there is a conversation which many job applicants are not aware is occurring between themselves and their interviewer. Have you ever been asked a question by an interviewer and wondered, how does this have anything to do with the job I am applying for? I am sure we have all been asked questions that appear as though any answer would paint you in a negative light. What if, instead of trying to trap us by our answers, the interviewer is really giving us an opportunity to display a strength? What if that interviewer does not care as much about the answer to the question as the logic and insights our response displays?

Some of the most notable interviews in the nation occur at the National Football League's annual scouting combine. Every year analysts and pundits remark at the seeming absurdity of the questions asked potential players. A few of the more ludicrous include, "Do you wear a G-string or jock strap when you play?" "How many different things can you think of that you can do with a paperclip?" and "Do you picture yourself as more of a dog or a cat?" The players and commentators echo the same sentiment: What does any of this have to do with playing football? In fact, many were offended at the questions being asked, and vocalized their agitation with the team and the interview process as a whole.

Now I don't know if those players pictured themselves as more Garfield or Odie, or if their in-game attire came from Victoria's Secret or Dick's Sporting goods, but I do know that they failed that particular test. NFL interviews are not intended to determine who can throw a 20-yard out the most accurately, or who is better at filling the C gap against a zone read. In fact, the players are correct, these interview questions have nothing to do with on-field ability. That is what film is for, or in most of our cases that it what our resumes are for.

What these players and the author of the piece didn't realize was that the task potential employees will be paid to do is only one part of what future employers assess during the interview. How is this person going to interact with the other members of this team? Is he going to listen and follow supervisors' directions? How does he respond when confused, insulted, or surprised? Most importantly, if I hire this person, how will their actions reflect on me and my organization.

When we realize what the interviewer is actually trying to accomplish, we can translate what was actually said to what is really being asked:

What was said: "Do you wear a G-string or jockstrap when you play?"

What was asked: "You have been given special treatment your entire life because of your ability to play football. No one has insulted you because you are 300 pounds of muscle and could rip in half anyone who said something you didn't like. As a member of our team, you will be subjected to the media's second-guessing your decisions, questioning your toughness, and trying to elicit a reaction from you. If you overreact, it is going to make our entire organization look like arrogant hotheads. How can we be certain that you will not cause a scene that our public relations department will have to clean up?"

So now that we know what the real question is, how do we answer it effectively? The worst response is to blow up on the interviewer or asking, "What the hell do you think?!" If, however, you respond with a straight face, or even worse, a look of indignation as you state that you wear a jock strap. This can be interpreted as your having no personality. This is not necessarily a strike against you, but your answer does nothing to separate you from the field. If you answer "G-string," you may be assessed as disrespectful to authority.

The best approach to this question is to avoid the trap of actually answering it. What if, instead, you let out a slight chuckle to acknowledge that you don't take yourself too seriously and understand why they are asking the question? Then you respond with, "I prefer a low rise bikini – silk if possible, as it prevents chaffing." In that response what you really said was, "I have a personality that will endear fans to me. I can think on my feet when put into a trap situation, and, most importantly, I don't have any hot buttons for the media to push on a slow news day."

Now your future career may not involve you interacting with bored reporters trying to poke the proverbial bear, but from this example we can see a universal truth. The information your interviewer is trying to obtain about you is not necessarily reflective of the literal questions they ask. When you hear, "Tell me your biggest failure." you can bet that the questioner really wants to hear how you deal with failure and grow from it, as opposed to learning how much you cost your last employer when you burned down the warehouse. If you hear, "What do you consider your greatest achievement?" What they really want to know is how you measure success and what do you value as an individual.

In my career as a sales professional, I have studied and developed this ability to listen and translate what customers say to me in order to fully understand what they really want. Through working with friends and family who were facing growing challenges in the job market, I discovered that this skill that enables me to close sales is the key differentiator in determining who gets hired and who continues searching.

To tailor this system to the interview process, I worked with numerous recruiters and hiring managers to determine what questions candidates are commonly asked and what information interviewers truly seek when they meet with a prospective employee. Through my research I learned that although there is a litany of potential questions, they all point to two "big" questions the interviewer trying to wants answered:

1. Is this person a good fit for the job? That is, are you able to perform the tasks required and fit the culture of the organization?

2. Is the job a good fit for this person? Will this person be passionate about the position and their performance, or are they going to be looking to move on shortly after they are hired?

Every answer you give should address one of these two questions, otherwise you have missed an opportunity to cement yourself as the only candidate they can logically select.

Now before we go any further I want to emphasize the three most important parts of any interview: PREPARATION. PREPARATION. PREPARATION. This book will teach you how to decipher what information interviewers are probing for with every question they ask. It will also teach you how to answer and deliver information that will resonate with your interviewer long after you walk out of their office. However, you will need to take the time to reflect on and craft responses that are uniquely your own before you ever meet your interviewer. When I was in the job market and transitioning out of the military, I worked with a recruiter named Dan McCall from Lucas Group. Dan was the epitome of a professional in this industry, and if you are lucky enough to work with someone half as helpful as Dan, you are sure to find the right position for you in no time. Dan shared with me a secret to interviewing that perfectly sums up the interview process. He said that in the interview you are "presenting your best self." In other words, he way you answer each question must be uniquely you. You can't use canned answers that describe someone else or some fictional "benchmark" job candidate; you need finely tuned and polished answers that are your own. At the end of each section of this book you will be asked to come up with at least five different stories, anecdotes, or examples to answer each type of question asked. Using these methods will ensure that your specific examples impress your interviewer, while conditioning you to have those examples ready and at your disposal when asked for them. Once your responses are fully polished, you will just have to practice identifying which category each of the questions your interviewer asks falls into. Remember, you must have multiple responses to each question type, as your interviewer will most likely ask more than one version of same big question.

With this book you will learn not only how to understand the interview's hidden language, but how to speak and leverage this language to your advantage. Instead of walking into interview traps you will be able to spring them on your future employer and separate yourself from the herd. When someone asks you how the interview went, you won't have to respond with "we'll see" or "they should get back to me soon." You will know exactly where you stand no matter who you are up against. Let's look at how you can stop being a passenger in the process and take over the driver's seat in your next interview by changing the game.

Chapter 2

Tell Me a Little Bit About Yourself

The first line of inquiry that we will discuss is a typical lead off question, and we will refer to it as the "Tell me a little bit about yourself" category. This type of questioning can come in many forms. You will probably be asked to "Walk me through your resume" or "Why do you think that you would be a good fit here at ACME?" This type of question can appear more industry-specific and take the form of "Why do you want to be in management?" or "What made you choose the software industry?" This question can even be forward looking, such as "What are some of your personal goals?" These types of questions are relatively easy to identify because they will be very broad and phrased in a way that makes them seem like your interviewer is trying to get to know you as a person rather than an applicant.

No matter how questions are phrased, the interviewer is seeking the same two pieces of information. Specifically, are you a good fit for the company, and is the company a good fit for you? To break this down one step further, how has your life up until now made you uniquely qualified to succeed in this position? Why will you be passionate about staying with this company long after we see a return on investment from hiring you?

I realize that this type of question may seem conversational, but do not fall into that trap. The other lines of questioning that we will discuss, will clearly be part of a process used to evaluate you. When someone asks you "What is your greatest strength?" or "Tell me about a time that you succeeded when you didn't think you could." they tip their hand that your response will be used to determine your ability to perform the job you are applying for. However, when someone asks you to tell them a little bit about yourself, you may be tempted to interpret it as small talk. We tend to relax and let our guard down when we hear these kinds of questions because they seem just as likely to come up in a casual conversation with new acquaintances as they would in a job interview. As a result, candidates tend to be less precise with their wording and message. They not only miss an opportunity to differentiate themselves from other applicants, but in this question more than any other they unknowingly sabotage their chances with their interviewer.

This point cannot be stressed enough. More people will remove themselves from consideration with their response to these questions than at any other time in the recruitment process.

How is this possible? How can a question that seems so innocuous actually disqualify you from consideration? How can a question that seems to have no wrong answers be what stops an otherwise qualified candidate from getting an offer? First, always remember that if it seems like there are no wrong answers to a question, it is because you are not picking up on what question is really being asked. Second, when an interviewer takes an intentionally lighthearted tone, they are doing so because they want to gather information from you which may prevent you from getting an offer without raising and red flags in your mind.

One recruiter I interviewed in researching this book shared with me one example of how this tactic works. He said that many interviewers will start a conversation with "So where are you from?" This seems like a simple pleasantry that is thrown out to establish rapport with a candidate. The reality, however, is that most people make career decisions based on location over any other factor. So if the candidate states that they have strong ties to certain geographical locations, and the job requires moving to another city or state at some point in the future, that interviewer will remove the applicant from consideration no matter how qualified they may be for the position. Even if the candidate is willing to move now, the interviewer is playing the odds that he or she will one day want to move back "home."

This example should serve as a crucial reminder that everything said in an interview will be used to evaluate a candidate. I realize that this is going to make most people very nervous. Most people will read that example and think there is no way they will be able to negotiate such a minefield unscathed. You, however, should be thinking just the opposite. If everything you say is being evaluated, then everything you say presents an opportunity to strengthen your position in the interviewer's mind. Let's look at the previous example. What if instead of talking about the city you grew up in where you currently live, you said something like, "Well most of my childhood I lived in Oklahoma City, but I went to college in Florida. I also visited family in New York every Christmas, so I kind of consider that as my second home." In this response you have not only made yourself more interesting as far as the conversation goes, but you have also expressed that you have ties all over the country and are therefore open to change should it be necessary.

Now that we know the true potential of these types of questions, let's take a look at how most people respond to them and how you can separate yourself from the crowd. First let's look at the common way people respond to the "Tell me a little bit about yourself" question:

"Well, I went to the University of Michigan where I majored in business management and graduated with honors. My first job out of school was with XYZ industries, where I was part of the operations team. There I was tasked with improving efficiency on the production line. I was able to implement several lean initiatives that saved the company over $100,000. From there, I went to A&G Inc., where I headed up the customer service team.

"During my time at A&G, I initiated several training projects for customer service team members that lowered average call hold time by 27 percent and reduced customer complaints by more than half.

"Currently, I am working with KP Corp. as a sales manager, where I manage five reps and over 30 different product lines. When I accepted my current position at KP the territory was at 82 percent of goal with two vacant positions. I was able to hire two great reps and successfully developed the territory to over six straight quarters over 100 percent of quota."

This seems like a great response, right? This person has shown that they have been successful everywhere they went. They have demonstrated aptitude in increasing levels of responsibility with obvious drive to progress their career. What's more, this candidate put tangible quantitative measurements of their success in every position. Wouldn't the interviewer conclude that this candidate would be a fantastic asset no matter what position they were offered?

What if I told you that is exactly what is wrong with this response? This candidate is perfectly qualified for any position, but they are not interviewing for just any position. They are interviewing for a specific position with a specific company. This candidate has only regurgitated information that is most likely already on their resume. Writing your resume in this manner makes sense because you will send out an identical resume to numerous companies as you apply for a variety of positions. In the interview stage, however, you are most likely competing with a couple other candidates whom the interviewer has also deemed qualified for the position. Therefore, reiterating why you are good enough to interview does not separate you from the other candidates. What's more, why would the interviewer be convinced that this candidate will not jump ship when another opportunity arises? Why should the interviewer believe that this candidate will be passionate about the role or company they are hoping to join? The interviewer is trying to determine the best fit for the position, and that fit goes both ways. Your response needs to tell them why only **you** are acceptable for this job, and just as significant, why only **this** position is perfect for you.

There is another problem with this response. It's not memorable. **If your responses aren't memorable then you will not be memorable**. You will just be another page in a stack of resumes that your interviewer sorted through or another face in the crowd of potential candidates. Without rereading the response, try to recall the second company this person worked for after graduating college. How much money did he save the company in his first position? Did the candidate convey why he wants to work for this particular company? If you can't remember this information shortly after you read the answer, what are the odds that the interviewer will remember it once they have conducted several interviews with other candidates?

The key to being memorable is to tell a story. Listing information makes that information very forgettable. It melts into a random assortment of numbers, dates, and facts that go in one ear and out the other. Creating a narrative, however, binds the information together into a single unit with purpose and direction. To think of it another way, why do people make shopping lists before they go to a grocery store? Each item on the list has a purpose and value to the individual, but there is nothing to unify all that information. Without the list, shoppers know they are likely to forget to pick something they need. Those same people, however, can probably quote lines from their favorite movie, even if they haven't seen it in more than 10 years. That's just the way our brains are wired. We are able to remember specific lines because they are part of a larger theme. They connect with each other as part of a larger purpose. Items on a list are not interconnected, but details of a story rely on each other to generate direction and reveal an ultimate goal.

Now, let's see how the same candidate's response improves when we add in purpose to every action to create a narrative about their life. As you read this response, think about how your opinion of the person changes. What qualities do you envision in this person? Do you think they will fit in with the culture of the company they are pursuing? Do you think they are likely to be driven to perform if they get the role? What is the likelihood they will leave quickly after being hired?

"When I was in high school, I was on the basketball team, and after tryouts I could tell we did not have a whole lot of talent on the team. Personally, I could not shoot a free throw to save my life. We did however, have a phenomenal coach. I will never forget him. His name was Coach Smith and he was able to pull every ounce of ability out of our team. He had an uncanny ability to develop us where we were weak, and at the same time create opportunities for us to showcase our strengths. He was the kind of person you would not want to disappoint because you could tell how much he cared about each player's and the team's success.

After my experience with Coach Smith, I knew what I wanted to do with my life. I wanted to be great at developing organizations and pulling the most out of a team. I chose to study business management at the University of Michigan because of that desire to learn teambuilding and leadership.

While there I tried to soak up as much knowledge as I could on how to be great at leading a team in the corporate world. One of the most important lessons I learned was that you can't be a great leader if you don't first learn what you are going to be asking your team to accomplish. That is why I joined XYZ industries for my first job out of college. XYZ has a great reputation for their manufacturing processes and are real innovators in process improvement. The knowledge I gained there was invaluable. I was able to learn best practices, implement my own ideas, and see firsthand how different tweaks have a ripple effect through the productivity and efficiency of the entire line. I really valued my time there, but I knew that in order to achieve my goal of being a leader I needed not only leadership experience, but also knowledge of how different departments within a company work together. So I took an opportunity to head up the customer service department at A&G.

"During my time there, I was able to witness the dynamic cooperation and see how decisions made on the production line affect customers. I also learned what services customers value from their vendors. I was able to apply lessons I learned in prior positions and explain them to my team so we could work as a cohesive company rather than distinct departments. I was also able to develop the interpersonal skills every great manager needs. After three years I was ready to take on a bigger challenge in a more dynamic leadership role. So that's why I joined KP Corp.

"As an industry leader in sales training, KP was the perfect landing spot for me. My job there gave me the opportunity to learn another crucial skill while continuing to expand my skills as a manager in a much more complex and demanding setting. I love my current position and the people I have the pleasure of leading. For a long term role, however, I want join an industry and a company that connect with me on a personal level. My father has struggled with diabetes his entire life. While I was doing some research for him I came across your company and saw the amazing things you have been able to do with your products. Immediately, I knew it was something I had to be a part of. I believe that in order to be successful, you have to be passionate about what you do. I can't imagine finding an organization where I would be more passionate to show up every morning than a place that is helping people like my dad."

Which of these two candidates do you want on your team? From the two responses, which candidate do you think will be more successful in the role? Both candidates have the same education and the same work experience, but the second one you can connect with. The second candidate answered the question "Who are you," while the first merely answered "What have you done?" The second interviewee gave a purpose for every decision he has made in his life. The second candidate told the story of why his entire life has been preparing him and leading him to this particular position.

Remember the two pieces of information the interviewer is trying to determine with every question asks: **"Are you a good fit for this job, and is this job a good fit for you?"** The first candidate answered the first question. He is clearly qualified for almost any position. The second candidate, however, explained why he would be a fit for the company, as well as why that company is the perfect fit for him. Let's look deeper at why. What motivated the first candidate? We don't know, but it would be safe to infer that he was looking to find a job with the most prestigious title or the highest pay. What would stop him from leaving when the next opportunity arises? What makes him passionate about the work? How do we know that he is going to make every effort to fit into the company's culture? The first candidate may be a great employee, but because he didn't give the interviewer an answer to that explained his motivations she could very well assume that he doesn't have any.

Let's dissect the second response to see what tactics our applicant used to convey why they were a perfect match for this company. The response starts with a quick anecdote about their high school basketball coach, and it accomplishes two goals. First, most people can relate to the story. Everyone has had a role model they looked up to and who left an impression on them when they were younger. The interviewer hearing this story will not think of Coach Smith, but rather the role model in their life. This immediately creates a personal connection between the interviewer and the interviewee. By implying that it was their life's goal to be like Coach Smith, the interviewee connects himself with interviewer's own role model from their past. What's more, the anecdote gives a reason for the interviewee to be passionate about being a good manager and to strive for self-development. The interviewer assumes that this passion will translate to overcoming any challenges that arise in the new role. The story also allows the candidate to express what qualities he thinks are critical to being a good leader or manager without appearing to brag. If you say that you value those qualities in someone else, the interviewer will believe that you work to create those qualities within yourself.

Next, we will examine how the candidate states he makes decisions. With each event in his life, the candidate details his motivations for each choice and how they drove him down a distinct path. Look at how he chose a college. He found a place where he could learn the most about leadership. How did he pick a first job out of college? He wanted to learn from a leading manufacturing processes company. He then left because he needed to gain leadership experience as well as learn other facets of a business to prepare to lead a team. Next he felt ready to gain experience on a larger level. Finally, he is looking for a spot where he can put everything he learned together in an industry he feels passionate about. Every change prepared him to thrive in this new position. No decisions were made based on money, location, or personal convenience. This tells the interviewer that the candidate is not only a great fit for the organization, but it also hints at how the candidate prioritizes his career. Every interviewer is watching out for candidates who view the job as merely a paycheck. If she believes the candidate will view the job as just a stepping stone or a means to an end, she will steer clear and avoid the headache down the line.

The candidate in this case describes every job in terms of what he learned while there. He does not just describe his successes. There are two reasons for this. First, all accomplishments at previous jobs will be on his resume. Restating them does not move him closer to being hired. In fact, when an interviewer hears information that she has already gathered, she begins to tune it out. This actually lessens the impact of those accomplishments in her mind. Second, describing what was learned at each position signals a humility that interviewers will fall in love with. People who are humble are much more likely to get along with their future coworkers than people who believe they have been great at everything they have ever done. Now think back to the "strengths" chapter. Isn't your interviewer more likely to believe you possess certain traits if you say how you learned and developed them as opposed to simply stating you have them mastered?

Now compare the tone of the two responses. How would you describe the tone of the first response? Would you describe it as upbeat? Would you consider this person passionate? Probably not. You would describe the first candidates' response as matter of fact or direct. If brutally honest, you might call it downright boring or lifeless. What about the tone of the second candidate's response? You would probably classify it as being very positive or optimistic. The second candidate seems to be the kind of person who sees the bright side of everything. He had something good to say about every job. Every experience seems to be a positive one, and not just in terms of accomplishments, but in how he felt about being there. A positive attitude about previous employers is a huge check in the "pro" column in the eyes of the interviewer. It indicates that this candidate will fit into the company culture. People with positive outlooks are much more likely to get along with coworkers and remain with a company throughout the inevitable ups and downs that come with any occupation. Conversely, if a candidate has a negative attitude about a previous position or employer, it will serve as a warning bell in the mind of the interviewer. Even if a candidate truly had a terrible boss or poor experiences with previous coworkers, she should never state that in an interview. The interviewer has no idea what really happened, and will assume that there are two side to the story. The interviewer will likely put themselves in the position of the previous employer and think, "If she had problems with managers or coworkers in her last position, then she will likely have similar problems in this role." At the very least the interviewer will think that there is a risk the person was in some way responsible for the issues at the previous position. She may simply decide not to take a chance on the applicant.

The final tactic that the second candidate employs which sets them apart is to make the narrative a personal story. The interviewer will see the first candidate as the one who saved X number of dollars at Y company or the one who made Z number of sales. The interviewer will only see them as numbers and statistics. It is very easy to say no to numbers and stats. Numbers and stats will be hired by someone, and numbers and stats will be just fine. Numbers and stats will probably forget that they even interviewed at this company a year from now. The second candidate, however, is not just numbers and stats. The second candidate is the person who dreams of leading a team that will help heal people like his father. By saying no to the second person that employer is not just saying they will have to work elsewhere. That employer is denying a passionate person their dream and calling. It is very easy to say no to an applicant. Applicants don't have feelings and emotions. *People,* however, do. It is very hard to say no to a person. It is especially hard to say no to a person once you made a connection with them. Every story and anecdote that the second candidate weaves into their response builds those connections with the interviewer and makes the interviewer see them on a personal level. Now the interviewer is not selecting between applicants, but rather between faceless applicants and a friend.

After reviewing how to address the "Tell me a little bit about yourself" style of questions, take some time to examine how you are going to respond. Remember, this line of questions can take many forms such as "Walk me through your resume" or "Why do you want to work for our company?" In reality they all are asking the same thing: "What motivates you?" "How do you make decisions about your life?" And most importantly, "Why are we a good fit for you and you a good fit for us?" Now think of at least five stories from your own life that illustrate who you are as a person and why that makes you and this position a perfect match. How will you weave some of these stories into your response? How did your previous experience mold you for this position, and how did they fit into your purpose for your life? You will likely be asked several versions of this question, so be prepared with a couple unique responses. Once you have those responses share them with someone you trust, and ask them to tell you what attributes they took away from your responses. Ask them what they learned about you on a personal level. Did they retain what you intended? If not, continue to rework your answers until the connections they make are the same ones you want your interviewer to pick up on.

Chapter 3

Good Times

The questions asked in every interview can be broken down into several categories. The next section we will look at is the "good times" question. This type of question can be about actual accomplishments or hypothetical situations. This category is your chance to brag about yourself (or so it would seem) and specifically your accomplishments. Using these questions as a means to prattle off stats and examples of your previous success, however, is falling into the interviewer's trap. Remember, the hiring decision will not be made on whether you cut your last budget by 20 percent or 40 percent. Nor will your interviewer call you back and say that the company decided to go with another candidate because at their previous job they were 110 percent of quota and you were only 105 percent of goal. No matter how great your accomplishments at your previous job, remember, no one cares what you did for someone else. They care about what you will do for them, and the circumstances of your future career will not be the same as the one you left. So let's take a look at what interviewers are really trying to learn by asking these questions, and more importantly, how to give it to them.

Whether you are asked "Tell me about your greatest success." or "Tell me about a time you overcame an obstacle that you didn't think you could." or "How do you work with a team?" your interviewer is actually asking you the same question. This may sound absurd to you. For example, you may be thinking that my biggest success was not part of a team, or I never thought that I couldn't achieve something at my last position. So how could each of these questions be answered the same way?

In order to answer that, as well as craft the appropriate response to these questions, we must first dissect what is at the core of this style of questioning. On its face, it would seem that the interviewer is saying "Please take the next five minutes to brag about yourself. Explain to me why your trophy collection is so expansive that I would be a fool to think you will be anything other than the greatest success this company has ever seen." Even the question, "How do you work with a team?" fits into this category because no one in their right mind would respond that they can't collaborate. It would appear as the only possible answer is that you work well with others. If the question seems like there is no wrong answer you can be certain that most common answers are wrong.

The interviewer knows that everyone they consider for this position will come from diverse backgrounds with different work experience. So how would they be able to know that if you were put in a similar experience as another candidate you would not perform just as well, if not better? If comparing results is impossible, then why even ask the question?

The answer is, these aren't the real questions they are asking. Your interviewer is not interested in what you have actually accomplished. They are, however, interested in how you are mentally and personally driven you to succeed, and just as important what you consider a success. They need to know, "Is this person I am hiring only concerned about her own personal gain, or does she care about making the organization better?" They want to know if you set your own goals, or if you only measure success by achieving goals others set for you. Do you measure the value of an achievement by the size of the result or by the amount of effort expended? The way the questions are phrased put the emphasis on what you have done in the past, but your answer needs to focus on how the traits you possess will translate to success in the future of their organization.

Let's take a look at a few responses to these questions that demonstrate the right way, the wrong way, and the typical way to answer these questions:

First the wrong way. "Tell me about your biggest success or achievement."

"I achieved 120 percent of quota in the third quarter of last year. It was the most of any representative in the company."

This sounds like a great achievement that would indicate future success, but it does not cover any of the bases that the interviewer really wanted covered. What the interviewer heard was "My only goals (or at least the ones I care about) are the minimums that my employer sets for me. I do not take into account the contributions of others around me when I evaluate my success. I also don't care about what work goes into the process as long as I finish ahead of my teammates." In addition, this "story" is probably just restating something that appears on your resume. So how is your future employer supposed to take that information and translate it to your performance within their organization?

Now let's take a look at how most people will tell you to answer that question. Keep in mind that this is not necessarily wrong, but it won't separate you from the pack.

"Last year everyone on our sales team was in a bit of a slump. We lost a major account as a company and we weren't getting much traction with our prospects. So I sat down one day and wrote a plan of how I was going to start gaining momentum in my territory. The key to my plan was to use current customers as references for people who were still on the fence. I started setting up monthly dinners for current customers and prospects to meet each other and build relationships. The process started to take off and I was able to close 10 deals as a direct result. The system I utilized resulted in my attaining 120 percent of quota."

That sounds pretty good, right? It even follows the "STAR" method that I am sure you have been told about at some point in your interview preparations. You had a **situation** or **task**. You clearly stated the **actions** that you took as well as how those actions **resulted** in the accomplishment of a goal. This second answer seems like the individual is much more motivated and a self-starter than the first response. Plus, his actions helped the entire company. In fact, I am sure that you have read hundreds of responses that sound just like this in other interview preparation books. So what could be wrong with this response?

There are two main issues with this answer. First, *you have read hundreds of responses that sound just like this in other interview preparation books.* The point of an interview is to differentiate yourself from the competition. How can you do that if your answers sound just like everyone else's? The second issue with this response is that it only tells your interviewer what you have done and not who you are. Firms are trying to hire people with the personal attributes that will make them successful in the new role, not just someone who was successful in a previous role.

To illustrate this point let's look at what this response actually says about the person and why that is important. First, what was their biggest accomplishment? Reaching or surpassing quota. That sounds on its face like a good thing, but that is a goal that was given by management. What does it say about you if the goal that you are the proudest of is not one that you set for yourself? This could be interpreted as a lack of ambition or personal drive. Secondly, this accomplishment is a personal win. Again, that doesn't seem like a bad thing, but it can be interpreted as selfish or at least self-focused. Think about how the perception would change if the achievement that you were the proudest of was one where you helped someone else succeed? Who would you rather have on your team?

Ok, so we have seen the wrong way to answer the question and the way that everyone else will answer the question, but how should you answer it? As you read the following response try to see if you can interpret what the true message is.

"Well, I consider my greatest success to be convincing my wife to marry a schlub like me, but I assume that you are more interested in work related achievements. That is a tough question because I have been very blessed throughout my career. Although there is one thing that sticks out in my mind that I am very proud of.

At my last job, I had a fellow sales rep named Nick. Now, Nick was a great guy, and he knew our products like the back of his hand. In fact, I often would reach out to Nick if I had a technical question. Nick, however, always struggled when presenting to large groups. If he was speaking to a large audience, he would often get nervous and rush or forget where he was going.

If Nick could become more comfortable speaking in front of large groups of people, his potential would be unlimited. So after one of our meetings, I pulled Nick aside and told him that I appreciated all of the times that he helped me out, and if he was interested I would love to help him improve his public speaking skills. He was very grateful and agreed to work with me. Well, the first thing I did was share one of the books that I used when I was trying to develop my own public speaking ability. After he finished reading that, we developed a plan. He started practicing with me, and then in front of his family, and finally we joined a local Toastmasters club. It was great to see Nick develop his skills and gain confidence over all the hours of practice. Helping him also enabled me to refine my skills along the way. Last year Nick was selected to give a presentation to our entire sales staff at the national meeting. When it was his time to present, Nick performed flawlessly. As I watched him give his talk, I was amazed at how far he had come, and knowing that I was a small part of that transition was my proudest moment with the organization."

This response is probably a lot different than how you have heard this question answered in the past. Good! It should be. Remember, the interview is where you separate yourself from everyone else, and not where you compare yourself to everyone else. Let's delve deeper into this response to see why it sounds different from what you heard before as well as what the subtext of the response really communicates.

The first thing that should jump out at you is the tone. The tone of this response is conversational. If your response sounds canned or robotic, it will not be memorable, nor will it connect with your interviewer on a personal level. That connection is key to your success. People hire people they like. If your interview sounds like two friends reminiscing, as opposed to a sterile interrogation, you are on the right track. How do we achieve this tone? The first sentence of this response gets us off to a great start. First, it personalizes you by illustrating that you have relationships and motivations outside the office and that you are more than just a potential employee. Second, it is self-deprecating. This type of humor shows humility, that you don't take yourself too seriously. Subtle remarks like this can endear you to your interviewer as well as demonstrate an ability to think on your feet. Finally, leading with a remark like this one shows that you have heard and interpreted the question you were asked and not simply regurgitating a response that you think they want to hear. This makes your actual response carry more weight and be more believable.

Let's dissect the transition sentence that was used before we get into the real answer. By stating that you were "very blessed throughout your career," you actually accomplish a couple of objectives. First, with this sentence you make it clear that you have been a high achiever in all of your previous endeavors. What is more, you were able to do so while still sounding appreciative and not braggadocios. Secondly, this transition conveyed that although your personal success is important to you, it is not the only motivation that drives you. This response redirects a question that expects you to brag about yourself, into a statement about your desire to help other members of your team. This transitional sentence allows you to divert your response from telling your interviewer what you have done to describing who you are. Isn't that what your interviewer really wants to hear anyway?

This brings us to the meat of the response. Most people will tell a story about how they had to create a plan to accomplish a goal they thought they couldn't meet. They do this to illustrate that they are organized and have great forethought. Then they dive into how many hours of arduous labor they dedicated to achieving this goal in order to convey that they are hardworking. Finally, they reference some grandiose metric that demonstrate that they are incredibly successful and the lynchpin of their entire organization.

Now I want you to picture that friend, acquaintance, or coworker who is constantly bragging about themselves. We all know that person or have met that person at one time or another in our life. Whenever we come across someone like that, we all have the same response. We tune them out. No matter what the story is, once they start their rant, we start thinking about something else… anything else. What's more we usually minimize the importance of their achievement by at least half. I can guarantee that the interviewer is doing the same thing. He or she has been sitting through candidate after candidate explaining why they are the greatest thing since sliced bread, so regardless of your accomplishment this approach will not make you stand out in their mind.

Take a second to reread this response. Did it illustrate an ability to organize and plan? Did it outline dedication and willingness to work hard? Finally, did it demonstrate success and valuable to the organization? Absolutely, but it also did more than that. It made clear that you revel in the success of others instead of wallowing in jealousy when you are not the center of attention. It demonstrated that you are motivated by the success of the organization and not simply personal gain. This response indicates that when your interviewer makes the decision to hire you, your future peers will be glad they did instead of resent them for it. Remember, the resume tells the story of what you can do, but the interview is the time to tell your future employer who you are.

With this new knowledge of what really matters to your interviewer, it's time to practice. When your interviewer asks "What is your greatest success?" what is the real question you are going to answer? What personal attributes do you think are most important to your future employer, and how are you going to illustrate those through the story you tell? Once you decide on which of your experiences best fits the narrative you want to convey, determine different ways to modify your response so that it is applicable for any of the variations of the "What is your greatest success" question.

Now that you have your response crafted, share it with a friend or family member. Ask them what characteristics they gleaned from your response. If they are not the traits or attributes you were hoping to embody, rework your response until what you intended matches what was understood by your audience. This part is crucial to your success and is often overlooked. Always remember, it doesn't matter what you say. It only matters what the listener infers and what resonated. Also, ask your audience if they were entertained by your response. Being entertaining is important for two reasons. First, it makes you likeable and people only hire people they like. Second, if your story is entertaining it is much more likely to be remembered.

Chapter 4

Bad Times

The mirror opposite of the "good times" category is when your interviewer asks you to tell about a time that you came up short in your last position or what you would do if faced with a specific challenge in the new position. We will refer to these as "bad times" questions. These questions come in various wordings, but the substance within them is the same. They sound something like "Tell me about a time you failed to achieve a goal" or "What was your biggest mistake with your last employer?" This category of questions is one of the few times your interviewer will not be hiding the fact that the question is a trap. On the surface it would seem like your interviewer is looking for you to expose the skeletons in your closet so they can determine which candidate has the least dirty laundry. This thinking will often catch people off guard, and candidates will pick a small incident and explain why they were not really to blame for the issue. Even worse, some candidates will not come up with an incident to tell their interviewer. These responses would make sense if the interviewer were really trying to weigh the errors prospective candidates have made in order to find the "least bad" candidate. In that instance, the person with nothing negative on their track record should win... right?

If that were the case, why would the interviewer even bother asking the question in the first place? Obviously, no candidate would tell them something so blatantly irresponsible that it would prevent them from being hired. Conversely, no interviewer has ever offered someone a job on the spot after hearing that they did not make any mistakes at their last job. What insight could the interviewer hope to garner from this question? The answer to that question becomes apparent when we remember that the interview is not where your future employer learns what you have done, but rather who you are. So when you hear questions like, "Tell me about a time you failed" you should interpret that as, "How do you adapt to an obstacle?", "Are you easily frustrated?", "How do your interactions with coworkers change when stress is involved?", and most importantly "What have you learned from your mistakes?"

So if we replace this line of questioning with what is really being asked, how do the responses that most candidates give stack up? If you were asked "How do you adapt to an obstacle?" and responded with an insignificant mistake or failure, you are really telling the interviewer that you have never truly been tested. How can you demonstrate that you are not easily frustrated or affected by stress if you have never been put in a stressful situation? Worst of all, if the interviewer is trying to ascertain how you learn from your mistakes, what are you telling them if you can't even remember a mistake you have made?

As cliché as it may sound, everyone does make mistakes. If you attempt to downplay or hide yours, you will not only lose credibility with your interviewer, but you will miss another golden opportunity to separate yourself from everyone else. Take a second to think about the information we just determined that the interviewer is really seeking. What, in that interviewer's eyes, is the best possible response a candidate could give? Couldn't you argue that it would be a story about facing a failure where the stakes were larger than what they would expect to see in the new position and handling that failure with grace? What if there was a candidate who had already committed the error the interviewer was most concerned about an employee making and now has the lesson that comes with that error etched in their mind?

Let's break the possible answers down into the wrong way, the way everyone else will answer, and the way you should answer this question. First, we will take a look at the wrong way to answer the question. There are several wrong ways to go about this. I'll list a few of the obvious ones before we get into the more subtle wrong ways to answer. If you were fired for doing anything illegal or immoral at your last position this would obviously be the wrong story to tell. This should go without saying. Even if you learned from this mistake and plan on never repeating your actions, it's best to leave that out of the conversation because it would demonstrate a propensity for such actions.

Another example of an obviously wrong way to answer this line of questioning is the "There isn't really a failure of significance that comes to mind" response. As we discussed earlier, with this answer you are really telling your interviewer, "Not only do I not learn from my mistakes, I am either so oblivious or self-righteous that I can't even admit my failures." This response not only makes you seem incompetent, but more important, unlikeable because of the lack of humility it demonstrates. Likeability is one of, if not the most, important characteristics you need to demonstrate in your interview. If your interviewer sees you as someone they could be friends with outside the workplace, they will look past almost any shortcomings you may possess. By the same token, if your interview sees you as the person they will dread running into at the watercooler, it won't matter how competent or successful you are. They will hire someone else.

Now let's take a look at an answer that is sure to raise some red flags, but it may not be as obvious why:

"With my last employer, I was in charge of a team of 10 people. Most of them were great workers and we were very successful. The team was consistently meeting the goals the company set for us. There was, however, one team member named Tom. Tom continually came up short and required the rest of team to cover for his mistakes. Most of the time his performance was just a little below par. I let it go, as the team was performing well as a whole. At one point, however, we were working on an important project a hard deadline. Tom again failed to deliver what we needed from him. As a result, the whole project finished past due and over budget. This made the entire team look bad to the organization, and I had to fire Tom. I should have paid attention to the warning signs earlier and found a replacement for him before we had such an important project thrown our way."

On the surface this response seems like a manager telling a story about how he learned to be more decisive. This answer does state a failure that may come up in your future position and recounts a lesson that you took away from it. Isn't that what you try to make clear to the interviewer?

In this instance that is not the only message your interviewer will take away from the response. First and foremost, the interviewer asked for **your** failures, not Tom's. This response really says, "I don't really believe that anything is my fault, and if the team that I manage comes up short I will always look for a scapegoat." As we stated before, in the interview it does not matter as much what you have done, but rather who you are as a person. This example may be the event that cost the organization the most money, productivity, or time, but believing that your biggest failure was not punishing someone for their shortcomings doesn't say much for your character. Nor does it paint the picture of someone who will immediately hit it off with their peers or subordinates.

The case of an underperforming team member is one that will likely appear in every managerial role. As a result, what separates a good manager from a sub-par one is the ability to rehabilitate underachieves and get the most out of them. Nowhere in this response did you state what efforts you made to coach Tom or incentivize him. Since replacing an employee is one of the most expensive options for an organization, this response actually says the lesson learned was to take an option that may be costly to the organization as a whole in order to put yourself in a better light. Ultimately, letting Tom go may have been the correct choice, but you will not be able to convince your interviewer that in the few moments you have to answer the question. The better choice would be to pick a story in which the lesson you learned is one that is undeniably beneficial to your future organization.

So now that we know the common pitfalls in answering this line of questioning, how do we capitalize on the opportunity that this question presents? The first step is to put yourself in the position of your interviewer. If you were looking at potential candidates, what is the one lesson you wish they would have learned before joining your organization? Obviously the answer will differ depending on your career, but take a second to determine what would be the most valuable lesson for someone in your field. Also try to think of a lesson that may be uncommon for someone in your position. This will not only make you seem more valuable, but also distinguish you from those you are competing against for the job.

Once you have the lesson picked out, you need to determine which of your qualities are most important to make clear through your story. Do you remain calm under pressure? Are you able to communicate effectively with both superiors and subordinates? When an issue arises, are you able to work through possible solutions logically and analytically to arrive at the best course of action? This should be the meat of your response that fits onto the core of the lesson that you learned. This is critical because everyone will have a lesson that they will be able to state to their interviewer, however, it is the qualities that the interviewer perceives in us that will separate us from the herd. I choose the phrasing "what the interviewer perceives" specifically, because if you simply state that you possess these qualities it will not resonate with your interviewer. They will often forget that you stated those qualities as they move on to ask the next question. So, if you are not supposed to state these qualities of yours, why did you need to pick them out before crafting your response? You picked out these qualities because every anecdote, every phrase, and every expression that you include in your response should be used to demonstrate these qualities. This is because your interviewer will remember the stories you tell much more than any statements you make. What's more, they will remember how the story and the way you told it, made them feel about you. How they feel about you is what will ultimately earn or lose you the job.

Here is an example of the right way to answer the "Tell me about a time you failed question." As you read this response, see if you can pick out the qualities and lesson that the candidate is trying to reveal with the response.

(With a slight laugh and briefly looking downward) "Well there is one that has really stuck with me. I was put in charge of production of a new product line at my last employer. This was a big deal at the time because the company was expanding quickly and the new product had to be ready for delivery in a very short time in order to meet the customer's needs. Also, we knew if we stumbled out of the gate it would be very difficult to get new customers on board or regain any customers that were lost because we were unable to deliver. So I started my plan by asking the advice of anyone and everyone in the organization who had experience relating to what we were trying to accomplish. Once I had the outline of my plan together, I gathered my team to go over it with them and fine-tune our next steps. As we were working on the plan, I noticed that we could cut production time if we unpacked all the raw materials at once instead of shutting down to do it as we went along. So I told my team to unpack everything on the first day in preparation for assembly later on. Once underway, I tracked our pace throughout the process. I quickly discovered that I was a little too ambitious with the speed I thought we would manage. This created a problem for us. We could no longer store the unpacked raw materials for an extended period of time. So I was left in an unenviable position. We were going to lose all of the raw materials we had on hand, be forced to order more, and miss our deadline, or run the risk of presenting a poor quality product as a result storing the materials improperly.

I called my director and explained the situation. I told him that I believed we had three alternatives. We could continue as we were and end up possibly producing an inferior product. I deemed this option unacceptable. We could scrap the raw materials I had unpacked, order more, and push back our deadline. This would be an expensive option for the company and the customers would not be enthused about having to wait for delivery, but we would be able to maintain our reputation for quality. I explained that although I believed this option to be tenable, it was not the path that I would recommend. The final option that I presented, was to authorize overtime for the members of my team and a new rotation of shifts that would allow us to continue production 24/7. I explained that this option would be expensive for the company, and the team would not be overly excited about the additional workload they would have to shoulder. But I believed that we would be able to maintain quality and meet our current deadline. After a bit of back and forth, the boss agreed to authorize the overtime. I then explained to my team the situation my miscalculation had put us in. I apologized to them, and asked their help to accomplish our goal. I could not have been more proud of my team at that moment because every one of them volunteered to work overtime and switch shifts in order to ensure that we met our deadline. Ever since, I have realized that when making a plan, you really need to understand why a process is done a certain way before changing it. Unfortunately, it was a rather expensive lesson, but one that I will not soon forget."

What qualities do you gather about this person from this response? Did the lesson seem like a valuable one? Is the way this person acted, the way you hope your employee would act in a similar situation?

Let's scrutinize this response, see what messages were delivered, and discuss why they are relevant to your interviewer. Right off the bat, the candidate expresses a slight laugh and a quick look downward. This expression demonstrates a visceral response to the memory as well as honest humility about what occurred. This is important as it sets the story up as an important memory that influenced the candidate, but also builds intrigue with the interviewer. This arouses the interviewer's curiosity about the response and commands her attention. Next the candidate states that he and his team were selected for this important role. This again is key because it shows that they earned enough respect in their organization through a track record of success to be placed in such a critical role. The candidate then sets up the challenges of the role as well as its importance to the organization. This outlines why the issue would be a particularly difficult one and the stress expected when the candidate faces the inevitable challenges. Remember, if you pick a relatively trivial error your interviewer will not value your response to the challenges it created.

Now that we have the background clearly established, let's look into the actions the candidate took. He states that he began by asking everyone he believed could be helpful for advice. What the interviewer really hears with this statement is "I am humble enough to know that I don't have all the answers when faced with a problem. I also have a personality that endears me with my colleagues in a way that they are happy to help. I am also a meticulous planner who does not jump into projects without foresight and preparation." The candidate then explains that he pulled in his team during the planning phase. This demonstrates that he is adept at leading others and has the ability make the team feel like it was not only his plan, but theirs as well. This leads to greater buy-in from every member.

Next, we get into the candidate's mistake. In this case the actual mistake was being too aggressive in pursuit of solutions. What do you think the interviewer took away from this mistake? Couldn't the candidate really be saying "I analyze every part of a given process to look for ways to improve?" Couldn't the interviewer see this candidate as a critical thinker who is not afraid to take risks? With this example, although the action resulted in failure, the attributes of the person who made this decision are positive ones. What's more important, the candidate takes full responsibility for the error. The cause is always stated as "my decision" or "I was overly ambitious." The quality of taking responsibility for one's actions is the single most important attribute you can present in answering the "bad times" line of questioning. This is because it is one of the most powerful predictors of future success in any endeavor, and your interviewer is sure to be looking for it in you.

The next section of the response details exactly what the candidate did once he realized he made a mistake. In this part of your response you will want to weave in as many examples of the qualities you have chosen to highlight. How many qualities about the candidate did you take away from this section of the response? Let's take a look at these together. The candidate states that the first step they took was to let their director know exactly what was going on and the challenges it was creating. This demonstrates that he does not shy away from taking responsibility, and that he keeps his superiors informed even when the news may have negative consequences. This behavior is exactly what a manager wants to see in the people they hire. The candidate takes this one step further in his response by stating that when he took the news of the problem to the director, he also shared possible solutions, including the course of action he recommended and eventually adopted. Coming to your superior with solutions when stating a problem demonstrates several key characteristics that your future employer wants. First, it shows that you are able to remain calm and logical when faced with adversity. It also shows determination in that you do not throw in the towel and start asking for others to solve your problems for you, but rather continue to work toward achieving the desired goal. The candidate explained the options including the pros and cons of each choice. This gives the interviewer a look inside the candidate's head to see what his priorities are and how he makes decisions. In this instance the candidate demonstrates that he is customer focused and unwilling to sacrifice the quality of the product and reputation of the company. He knows that the choice he recommends will be hard on the team, but his leadership will be enough to gain buy-in and complete the task. The candidate also states that there was "a little back and forth" between he and the director. This shows that the candidate is able to discuss options with his superior in a respectful manor, but still stand behind what he believes to be the correct choice.

The candidate goes on to describe how he interacted with his team once the decision was made. In the response he states, "I apologized to them," which again reiterates that he is able to take responsibility for his actions. In addition, it shows the candidate's ability to build a rapport with his subordinates. The strength of this rapport is demonstrated when the candidate states that everyone on the team volunteered to work overtime to make sure the project was a success. Isn't this the kind of relationship a future employer would love to see between a manager and his team? This candidate is able to convey that strength while telling the interviewer about a failure. Now that is how you separate yourself from the competition!

Last but not least, the candidate recaps the lesson they learned from this experience. This is crucial because you do not want your interviewer to misinterpret what you learned from this experience. If you do not state what you learned they could easily believe that you no longer take risks or no longer look for ways to improve. This candidate clearly states that he learned to always know **why** something is done a certain way before changing it. He did not say never change, or accept that the conventional way is always correct, but rather that when making changes the first step is to understand the purpose. No matter what the occupation, that is a great lesson that all employers would hope that their future employees would know from day one. This candidate not only stated that he learned that lesson, but also why it will stick with him in the future.

After reading this chapter, take a minute to review how you used to answer questions like these. What qualities did you express about yourself with your responses? What lesson would your previous interviewer say you learned from those experiences? Why will your interviewer remember the story you told? Now think about how you will answer these questions differently in the future. Will you use a different experience, or are there more parts to the story you will now choose to include? How will your tone or expressions differ after what we discussed in this chapter?

Chapter 5

Strengths

The categories of questions in the first two chapters of this book asked you to describe experiences. From the stories you tell, the interviewer attempts to interpret the qualities you possessed in order to determine how you would fare in the role they are hiring to fill. In the next categories of questions, however, the interviewer is going to cut to the chase and have you tell them exactly what qualities make you a fit for their organization. Or at least that is what it will appear they are doing with this line of questioning. As I am sure you have gathered at this point, the answer to the question they ask is not what they really want to hear, or at least it is not the question you should be answering.

This chapter will study the "strengths" line of questions. These are the questions that typically sound something like "What is your greatest strength?" "What qualities do you believe will make you successful here?" or "What made you want to be in this line of work?" Much like the "good times" line of questioning, this seems like an open invitation to brag about yourself. In fact, you are probably already mulling over a list of buzz words like "detail oriented" or "self-starter" in order to craft a response that can squeeze the most clichés into a single sentence. Therein lies the problem. They are clichés for a reason. Every candidate is going to tell the interviewer they should be selected because they are diligent hard workers, who sweat the small stuff because they are driven to achieve greatness by thinking outside the box while going the extra mile. All of these responses will go in one ear and out the other.

A simple interpretation of the question "What are your greatest strengths?" would be to translate that question to sound like "What strengths do you believe are necessary for this role?" This is the question most people chose to answer when responding to this line of questioning, but there are two problems with this approach. The first issue is the same thing we have been harping on: the purpose of the interview is to differentiate yourself from the other candidates, not mimic them. If you choose to answer the same question as everyone else how can you separate yourself from them? The second issue with electing to answer the "What strengths do you believe are necessary for this role?" question is how to convince your interviewer that you possess those strengths?

Let's think about that second issue this way. We have all come across the friend or coworker who loves to brag about themselves. Sometimes it's the meathead who rants on and on about how they live in the gym and can bench 400 pounds. Sometimes it's the wannabe American Idol who claims to have perfect pitch and "just killed it" at karaoke night last week. Maybe it's the salesmen who watched Glenn Gary Glenn Ross too many times and slips into every conversation that he is 200 percent of quota. No matter which version you hear, we all do the same thing. We mentally reduce them by about 50 percent. It is an almost innate response to pull others' proclamations back to the mean. There can be several causes for this. Maybe it's simple disbelief, or maybe it's because of our distaste for arrogance. No matter what the reason, you can be assured that your interviewer is doing the same thing when you rattle off your "greatest strengths."

I know that this seems like a catch-22. If your employer is going to downplay any strengths you claim to have because everyone exaggerates their strengths, wouldn't you then have to exaggerate your strengths even further so they come away with an accurate assessment of your ability? If you do overstate your strengths, isn't your interviewer even less likely to believe you? What if I told you there was a way to state your exact capabilities so your interviewer exaggerates them in their mind based on the way you answered the question?

This is absolutely possible when you change the question you are answering from "What are your strengths?" to "What abilities do you value?" "Why do you value them?" and "How do you work to create those abilities within yourself?" The last part of that question is the most important. By expressing the passion you have for improving yourself through details about the effort you put into honing your skills you will have the interviewer rooting for you to succeed.

Think about it this way. Call to mind any universally loved athlete. Specifically, try to think about someone who is regarded as one of, if not the greatest to ever play their sport. For example, look at Michael Jordan, Wayne Gretzky, or Peyton Manning. No matter who you picked, I am willing to bet there is a common phrase said about them, "They worked harder than anybody else" or "They were the first ones to arrive at work, and the last ones to leave." Whenever we hear these phrases two things happen. First, we start to want great things for them, and second, we double our perception of their ability in our minds.

Conversely, think about any athlete who is widely loathed or hated. Barring anyone who is hated for actions that took place off the field (illegal or otherwise), there is typically a theme that runs through the criticisms they face. That theme involves comments such as "overrated" or "wasted potential." We often hear that they were unwilling to put in the time and effort necessary to win. Take for example the story of Allen Iverson. Allen had phenomenal talent, and was quite possibly one of the best basketball players in history. However, we all remember him for the "We're talking about practice" quote. He made one statement that showed unwillingness to put in the extra effort to develop his skills, and the nation was aghast. The country quickly forgot all the wins, the points he scored, and the records he broke, and relegated him in the public eye as a disappointment. The problem with his statement regarding practice was not only that it showed a lack of commitment to his teammates, but it put into everyone's mind the idea that his skills and abilities were not attained through hard work and determination but were simply an innate gift. This is most likely not the case. One does not rise to the level of success that Iverson reached without putting in countless hours of work and practice, but it doesn't matter. As a result of one comment all that effort was written off. This is because whenever we believe that someone is born with an ability instead of acquiring in through rigorous effort, we not only downplay in our minds the scope of that ability, but we also diminish its perceived value.

If we don't want our interviewer to diminish the value of our strengths, then how are we supposed to answer a question that asks us to list our natural abilities? The secret is not answering the question "What are your greatest strengths?", but actually responding to "What strengths do you deem most important for success in the position you are applying for, and how do you continue to cultivate those strengths within yourself?"

The change to this question is significant for several reasons. First, it allows you to choose the strength that you want to discuss depending on what you believe your interviewer wants most in the people he or she hires. Your greatest strength may be your impeccable grammar, or your ability to hit a curveball, but those are not likely to help you land the position you seek. In choosing to describe the strength that you believe will be the most important to possess in order to be successful you are also telling the interviewer that you have insight and an understanding of the industry you are entering.

The second way changing the question you are answering is significant, is that it gives you the opportunity to explain how you attained that strength. Just as the example of the athletes we described previously, if you detail how you attained that strength and all of the effort it took to develop it, your interviewer will magnify their perception of that strength in their mind. What's more, you will demonstrate to your interviewer that you have the drive and ability to develop any skills that are required to be successful. This is paramount because no matter the job, you will have to be trained on how the organization expects you to execute your tasks. Your interviewer knows that regardless of how much experience you have in a given field, you will have to be trained in their specific methods. It is guaranteed that they are evaluating potential candidates for their aptitude to learn and develop. Answering this question is an opportunity to show your willingness to accept new ideas and a desire to grow professionally.

Finally, the correct way to answer this line of questioning shows that developing this strength is ongoing. This part is crucial. If you tell your future employer that you have this phenomenal ability, then every action you take involving that ability will come under scrutiny. For example, if you list your greatest strength as having attention to detail, then the first typo you overlook will make your employer second guess that you truly possess that ability. The employer may think you were dishonest in your interview and inject doubt into all your interactions with them. On the other hand, if you state that you have been working to instill an attention to detail within yourself, your employer will see any missteps as simply stumbles on your journey of development.

Now that we have established the question you should be answering, let's take a look at how the right way to answer this question compares to the way everyone else answers it. For this comparison we will use the same strength in our answer. After reading these two answers think to yourself which person you would rather hire and why. Think about which person you believe more strongly. Try to identify what other attributes you see in the person answering the question. First we will look at the standard way to answer the "What is your greatest strength?" question?:

"I believe that my greatest strength is my ability to communicate effectively. In my last position I was required to give very complicated and enormously detailed instructions to the team I was in charge of because the project we were working on required a very specific process to be followed in order to be successful. Before we began the day, I would bring my team together every morning to go over everyone's role in the project. I would have them ask me any questions they had, followed by a back brief where they would explain to me their understanding of what they were to do. We did this to keep everyone on the same page and the lines of communication open. As a result of this level of communication we were able to prevent any errors throughout the course of the project. In fact, we not only finished the project on time, but under budget as well."

Now let's take a look at how to answer when you change your response to fit the question you really want to answer:

"One day I was reading a book about General Patton and I came across a quote that really inspired me. He said, "Don't tell people how to do things. Tell them what to do and let them surprise you with the results." That was really powerful because it made me realize that the key to being a great leader or manager is not having all the answers, but rather being able to effectively communicate what we are trying to accomplish and why. So I decided that if I wanted to be more successful, I would need to develop my ability to communicate. In order to work on that, I started going to local Toastmasters meetings, as well as reading some books on the subject. I even took some improvisation classes to help develop my ability to think on my feet and communicate in a clear and effective manner. I think what was most effective was a book I read called *Crucial Conversations* by Kerry Patterson. That book helped me translate my thoughts into words in a much more precise and deliberate way. I can't tell you how much improving my ability to communicate has increased my productivity with my team and improve my relationship with them. I believe continuing to refine my ability to communicate will enable me to have a similar impact within your organization almost immediately."

If it were up to you, which of these two candidates would you hire? Both of these candidates said that the strength they possessed was their ability to communicate, but whom do you believe more? The first response follows the STAR method that many other experts will tell you to use when answering questions. That is to state a situation or task, the actions you took, and the results that came from those actions. When you hear this method used, however, it can feel cold and calculated. When you read that first response what emotions were triggered? Did you feel you liked that person? Was there a part of you that sensed the candidate was dedicated to his or her craft? Could you say definitively that the person who gave the first response was responsible for the success described, or could it be they were just in charge of a very strong team? Odds are you would have to answer, "I don't know" to all of these questions, and that is the exact opposite of the reaction that want to create in interviewers. They should know from every answer you give something about you as a person. They should be distinctly impressed by one or more of the attributes you expressed.

Now let's review the second response. Is there any doubt that this person has put in the work to become an exceptional communicator? What is more, think about all of the other attributes this person was able to exhibit. Is this person dedicated to self-improvement? Would you characterize them as open to learning new ideas? Is this person a hard worker and a self-starter? Clearly the person who gave the second response is all of these things, and you are more likely to believe it because they didn't come out and state these attributes explicitly. Rather the person in the second response gave you examples of actions that demonstrated these characteristics.

So how exactly did the second response elicit all of these reactions without expressly stating them? First off, the interviewee states that they were reading a book on General Patton. Let me state that again. They were READING a book. They were not watching a move, or a tv show, nor did they hear it from a friend. This matters because people who hire love readers. People who read for entertainment or self-improvement are seen as highly intelligent and possessing greater self-control than those who do not. Always weave in books you have read or are reading in your interview for just this reason. (That is unless the last book you read was *Fifty Shades of*

Grey or *Clifford the Big Red Dog*. Both those titles are likely to have the opposite effect to about the same degree.)

In the response, the interviewee also states that they were inspired by what they read and translated that inspiration to improvements in their career. This indicates that the interviewee was not motivated by previous failure nor a short term reward, but rather by an internal desire to better themselves. This is a critical trait that all interviewers are looking for, as it is a strong indicator of future success at any position. Discussing their inspiration for change, the interviewee explains their philosophy on management and leadership. In this manner they are able to sneak in another strength about themselves while seeming to only answer with one. While discussing why communication is such an important skill to possess, the interviewee actually said, "My management style is to give clear purpose and direction, while not micromanaging my subordinates." The interviewer will project that as, "My decision to hire this person will be supported by those I put him in charge of." This is another chief concern of the person who will be hiring you that you can mention without directly being asked.

Now let's take a look at the actions the candidate said they took to hone their skills as a communicator. The first thing to remember is that we said actions... as in plural. If you are trying to impart the amount of effort you put forth to develop a strength, then you need to list multiple courses of action taken to achieve it. Ideally, they should be both numerous and diverse in nature. This indicates that you are open to multiple methods of learning, and that you do not assume you are an expert just because you tried something once. This type of humility is very important in your interviewer's eyes. That is because they are almost certain to be training you in some form or fashion for your new role and they definitely do not want to bring on someone who read a single book and now thinks they are an expert on the topic. In this example the candidate stated ways that they learned about how to become a better communicator and ways they practiced these skills. A mixture of these two types of actions demonstrates not only cerebral development, but also a practical one. This candidate takes the opportunity to slide in another strength through their choice of methods to develop his ability to communicate. By using Toastmasters and improvisation classes as examples of how he practiced his communication, he is also telling the interviewer "I have learned how to use humor and social adeptness to endear myself to my future coworkers." This may be the biggest unspoken fear of your interviewer. No one wants to be the person who hired the guy that nobody likes. The candidate is able to double down on this strength by stating how the improvements in communication have improved his relationships with coworkers. Any way that you can instill confidence that you will get along with your future coworkers goes a long way to landing you the position.

In the final section of this response, the candidate is able to transmit two more key messages to the interviewer. First, the candidate makes it clear that personal development is an ongoing process. As we discussed earlier in the chapter, this goes a long way in setting proper expectations for your future employer. Now, if there are any issues in communication later on it will not affect your credibility with the person who hired you. There is another advantage in this phrasing, in that it shows your dedication to improving yourself as ongoing. The second message that the candidate was able to pass on to the interviewer was that the skills they have honed will be beneficial in this new role. This comment may seem like pandering, but in reality it shows that the candidate has analyzed of the position that they are applying for and has determine what will be required to be successful. Although this may seem like it would be understood, it is always beneficial to remind your interviewer how this skill will translate to the position you are after.

Now that you have seen the two example of how to respond to the "strengths" line of questioning, take some time to determine the strengths and abilities you believe are the most important to address with your future employer. Why do you believe those strengths will be crucial in the position you are seeking, and how have you gained those attributes? What actions have you taken to continue to sharpen those abilities? Are there any other strengths that you have that you want to convey to the interviewer? Write down a sample answer to this question and dissect what other messages you may be conveying.

Chapter 6

Weaknesses

Just as the "bad times" category of questioning is the mirror opposite of the "good times" category, there is a flip side to the "strengths" inquiries. That flip side is the "weaknesses" style of questions. We have all experienced this question in one form or another. Sometimes it's the obvious, "What do you consider to be your biggest weakness?" It could be more subtle such as, "What is something about yourself that you would change if you could?" No matter what the phrasing, the heart of the question is the same, and it is one of the biggest opportunities for differentiation that is almost universally missed.

To understand why most candidates will overlook this opportunity to separate themselves from the herd, we must first understand how they are interpreting the question. On the surface, this question looks like a trap. Most people think the interviewer is asking them for reasons they might not be successful in the position. Naturally, they begin to feel defensive and try to think of a weakness that will not be perceived as affecting their ability to perform. Often they will try to pick a weakness that everyone knows is really a strength. In doing so they believe that they have helped their case with the interviewer, because who wouldn't want to hire someone whose biggest issue is that they are a "perfectionist" or "workaholic who has trouble establishing a work life/balance."… Right?

If we unpack this line of thinking however, it doesn't really add up. Why would an interviewer ask someone to tell them their biggest weakness if the purpose of the question is to have the candidate say something that would exclude them from being hired? It would create a no-win scenario where if the candidate were honest (which should be what the interviewer wants) the company wouldn't offer them the job, and if the candidate lies, the company could end up hiring a dishonest person. Following this line of thought, it would seem like the interviewer is asking a question that they expect the candidate to lie about. So what answer would motivate the interviewer to move the candidate forward in the process? If the candidate contends that they do not have any glaring weakness that would prevent them from being successful, would the interviewer put a star next to their name because they would be a good fit, or mark them with an X because they believe the person was lying? What if the candidate admitted to a failing that would clearly create challenges if hired for the position? Would the interviewer be impressed with their honesty or eliminate them from contention because of their potential to struggle in the position? The real question you should be asking yourself is, "Why would an interviewer ask a question if the answer does not assist them in determining a potential candidate's value?"

The answer, of course, is that they wouldn't. That is not what they are trying to accomplish here. When the interviewer asks, "What is your greatest weakness?" what they really want to know is "What is your process for self-evaluation? How do you measure your own abilities, and when you find one lacking what steps do you take to improve it? How well do you take criticism? Do you possess humility or are your arrogant? Are you able to admit when you are wrong? Are you even able to recognize when you are wrong?" The answer to all of these questions is what they are trying to garner from your response. So in reality your specific weakness matters less if you are aware of it and you are taking steps to improve it.

The simple truth is that your interviewer knows you have weaknesses, what they want to know is do **you** know you have weaknesses. Take for example television shows such as *American Idol* or *America's Got Talent*. There are two things everyone wants to see when they turn on these shows. First, they tune in to see amazing performances from people like Kelly Clarkson and Carrie Underwood. Second, they tune in for the train wreck performances that would make a howler monkey buy earplugs. We can all see the allure of the great performances, but why would the show include the tone deaf wailings that seem more appropriate for a Yoko Ono concert than a talent competition? Viewers enjoy watching them not because the contestants can't sing, but because of their total lack of self-awareness. The reality is that most of us couldn't sing any better than those we are having a good laugh at. What we are mocking is the performers' hubris. It is this same hubris (although not on such a blatant scale) that your interviewer will try to identify in you when they ask the weakness questions. For that reason, one of the biggest mistakes you can make is to not be able to come up with a weakness you have identified in yourself or try to dodge the question by stating something as a weakness that both you and your interviewer know is really a strength.

We have established that you should not try to avoid the question. Does that mean that you should state an obvious failing that will inhibit your ability to perform the job? Absolutely not. If you are going for a sales position and state that you hate talking to people, or if you are an accountant who admits to inattention to detail these short comings will most likely get you shown the door. Remember **all** the questions that are actually being asked when the interviewer poses a weakness question. It's not enough to acknowledge that you have faults; you must also let them know how identifying and recognizing those faults has influenced you and what steps you have taken to fix them.

Let's take a look at how most candidates are coached to answer these types of questions:

"I think that one of the biggest weaknesses I struggle with is stubbornness. When I lock on to something I can't let it go until it's completed. I know that it drives my wife a little crazy sometimes, but it has also led to closing several deals that started out as "no's" from the customer."

This type of response follows guidelines that many interview coaches will give you. First, the candidate picks a weakness that affects an aspect of their life apart from work. In this instance the candidate states that his stubbornness is demonstrated in interactions with his wife. This is the candidate's attempt show awareness of the weakness and is not ducking the question, but his specific weakness does not affect his ability to do their job. The second guideline this candidate employs is framing a weakness as a strength. He does this by stating that stubbornness led to multiple successes in his previous job. This should be music to the employer's ears right? Who wouldn't want to hire a sales rep whose biggest flaw is that he doesn't take "no" for an answer?

The reality is that when interviewers hear responses like this, all kinds of alarms go off in their head. First off, the applicant's choice of stubbornness as his greatest weakness. When the interviewer hears that a candidate is stubborn, she interpret it as being difficult to coach or manage. It translates that the candidate does not adapt or learn quickly. Although the intent of using this weakness is to demonstrate persistence and candidate will not take "no" for an answer, all the future employer hears is that he will not take direction readily, will be difficult to manage, and might even defy his superiors. No matter what position you are going after, you will be expected to learn the company's methods and culture, so using a weakness like stubbornness can be a deal breaker for the potential employer.

Secondly, this candidate attempts to position his stubbornness as a weakness in his personal life that will not negatively affect his professional performance. This is another huge mistake on the part of the candidate. That is because one of the biggest aspects of a potential new hire that the employer is trying to determine through the interview process is how that candidate will get along with the company's current employees. If there is something about you that your spouse can't stand, what are the odds that your future coworkers will find it endearing? Finally, the candidate attempts to position this "weakness" as very beneficial in his career. This is an attempt at the "choose a weakness that is really a strength" tactic. Which is probably the worst way to answer this line of questioning. It completely misses the point of the question. The intent of the question is for the interviewer to get a feel for how well you identify your shortcomings and then understand your approach to mitigating or overcoming them. With those answers, you are really saying, "Not only am I not aware of my weaknesses, but I actually view what others call my weakness as a strength. Not only am I not open to change and growth, I will actively fight it because I believe that the things you would change about me are the reasons I am successful." Your future employer is not looking for someone who thinks they are perfect. They are looking for someone who is committed to self-improvement. An answer like this says that you are absolutely not that type of person.

Now let's look at the right way to answer this line of questioning:

With a slight chuckle, "Oh my biggest weakness has to be my terrible memory. Part of the reason I joined the military out of college was because they make everyone wear name tags. I think it might be clinically bad. It's why I carry this note pad with me at all times and I right down just about everything. I actually have to set alerts on my phone's calendar to review my notes every morning and create a checklist of things that I need to do and people I need to see that day. I don't know where I would be with my smart phone."

So why is this a good answer? Isn't having a terrible memory a big deal to a potential employer? Who would want to hire someone who is going to forget deadlines, or space out on the names of important clients? Having a bad memory could create a big problem no matter what the position. So why would you state that you have a weakness that is guaranteed to be a problem on the job?

The reason you would pick a weakness like this is precisely because it is guaranteed to have an impact on your potential job. Selecting a weakness that is neither here nor there in relation to the position that you are applying for shows that you are dodging the obvious intent of the question. In interviews, just like in politics, the cover-up is worse than the crime. If you elect to discuss a weakness that both you and your potential employer know will have no bearing on your ability to perform your job, they will think you are either unaware of your faults, or worse, that you are aware of them, and they are so detrimental that you think if the employer discovered them they would never offer you the position. Either way, you are raising a monumental red flag. There is another reason that a weakness such as a terrible memory is ideal for questions like this. It is an issue that everyone can relate to. No matter how good someone's memory is, we all think that we are forgetful. That's because we only notice our memory when it fails us. Go ahead and asks a couple friends and family members if they believe they have a good or bad memory. Almost universally, they will respond that they perceive their memory to be below average. Admitting that you have a bad memory is not only believable, but more importantly, people can relate. No employer will immediately write you off for having a weakness that they believe they have as well. Recognizing a common weakness humanizes you. In the employer's eyes you become more than just another candidate or resume. You connect viscerally and the interviewer begins to see you as a real person. It is easy to turn down a resume, but it is much harder to turn down a person.

Let's examine this response further, because choosing the right fault to share is only part of the correct way to answer the question. From the beginning, your answer must to set the correct tone that you will carry through your entire response. In our example, we do that with the "slight chuckle." What you are doing here is quite literally showing that you can laugh at yourself. In fact, that is exactly what the second line of the response does. Through joking about the weakness you possess you show that you have thick skin when it comes to discussing your faults. By setting a playful or relaxed tone you are showing that you do not take yourself too seriously, which translates to being open to hearing others correct or instruct you. This tone demonstrates that you can acknowledge your weakness, but it doesn't control you. By being relaxed when speaking about your weaknesses you are presenting a confidence that expresses your control over those faults.

So far, you have established that you are aware of your faults and that you are not sensitive about discussing them, but that won't get you the job. The next part of this response, however, will. Next you have to outline the process that you use to compensate for and overcome the faults you just described. This can be tricky. If you transition to this part of your response by saying something like "don't worry because I do X" or "I have overcome this weakness by doing Y." You create two issues. Your interviewer either will not believe you because when they hear these phrases the immediately believe that you are simply attempting to mitigate the damage done by stating a real weakness, or they wonder why you believe something you have overcome is still a weakness.

So how are you supposed to demonstrate how you overcame the stated weakness if you are not supposed to say that you overcame that weakness? Take a second to go back and reread the example of the correct way to answer the question. Does the candidate ever expressly proclaim that she has overcome the weakness? Or that the weakness has helped her in any way? No. Instead, the response lists the ways the candidate copes with the weakness as a means to drive home the severity of the fault. This method of saying "it's so bad that I have to X," however, has the opposite effect. Think about it this way. While reading the response did you think to yourself, "Wow, that person has a truly terrible memory"? I would be willing to bet instead you found yourself thinking, "That person has a great system. I should start doing some of those things." That is because the attitude that this response evokes is one that says, "I don't look at adaptation to my weaknesses as optional." When you use phrases like "this forces me to X or I have to do Y" what you are really telling your future employer is "I don't make excuses for myself" and "I am results-focused, and not driven by what is easy or convenient."

This method is much more likely to resonate with your employer than the "This is how I overcame this weakness" approach. Think back to the chapter on the "What's your greatest strengths question." How do people innately respond when you begin listing your strengths? They immediately begin depreciating in their mind the value of the strengths you state. Just as when you hear the meathead who brags that he can bench press 400 pounds and you mentally cut that number by thirty percent, your employer will do the same mental math when you boast about your strengths. In this situation, use this to your advantage. When people are self-deprecating, we automatically reduce the severity of their weakness in our minds. So when you use slight hyperbole in describing your weaknesses your interviewer will think to themselves, "It's probably not as bad as they are stating. In fact, I am sure that the weakness that this person is describing is just on par with everyone else." Therefore, by not making overt attempts to hide our shortcomings what we really do is induce the future employer to downplay them for us.

Finally, stating your weakness in this manor shows that it is an ongoing struggle. This is key because it will buy you some leeway once you actually have the position. Just like discussing how you are working to improve your strength improves your credibility when you actually have the job and are expected to display that strength, stating your methods to cope with your weakness will work to soften the repercussions if the weakness causes a hiccup later on. If the candidate who gave the above response lets something slip her mind while on the job, her employer is more likely to be understanding because she was upfront about the weakness in the hiring process and that employer knows that she is taking steps compensate. Conversely, if the candidate stated that she had overcome that weakness, the employer will begin to doubt her credibility when the fault appears.

Now that you have seen what right looks like, take a minute to craft how you will respond to this line of questioning. What weakness will you discuss? Are you bad at spelling? Do you have difficulty keeping track of time in your head? How are your mental math skills? All these are great examples of weaknesses that everyone thinks they suffer from, and you can easily describe steps that you take to cope with these shortcomings. What steps have you taken to deal with your chosen weakness? How will you state those steps in a manner that will resonate with your future employer? What statements will you use to set the tone of your response and express that you can laugh at yourself and readily take criticism? Write down a few sample responses to this line of questioning and pick apart the different messages that you may not be aware you are sending to your potential employer. It is important to have several responses ready, because if your interviewer is any good their second question will be, "What other weakness to you see in yourself?"

Chapter 7

Quick Hits

We analyzed how to interpret the most common categories of questions you are likely to face in an interview, provided the information that your interviewer truly wants to obtain, and showed how to provide it in ways that will resonate. In an interview, however, the questions your interviewer asks are only one of the many ways that you will be evaluated. In fact, many candidates will eliminate themselves from evaluation as a result of something that has nothing to do with their response to a question. In this section we will explore some of the most common ways people derail their interviews and how to avoid or even capitalize on them.

- Sweat The Small Talk

The first opportunity we will discuss happens the second you make eye contact with your interviewer. The opportunity we are talking about is the "small talk." Small talk will determine the tone and interviewer's mindset for the duration of your interaction. It is the first impression through which the rest of your conversation will be viewed. Yet, most people will completely ignore this chance to endear themselves to their interviewer. They will throw out a cliché or platitude such as "How are you?" or "Nice to meet you" while shaking the interviewer's hand and then wait for the first question to be asked. They will sound just like everyone else and become completely forgettable. If you want to be remembered and stand out from the other candidates, you need to put in more effort than the other candidates.

So how do you stand out with something as simple as small talk? You research. You research. Once you have done that, you research some more. Look up your interviewer on LinkedIn and Facebook. (you can be certain they are doing the same thing to you.) See what is important to them. Where are they from? Where did they go to school? Are they wearing a team's logo in any of their pictures? What is their title at their current job? What projects are they working on? What awards have they received in the past? Look up the company's S-1 on the SEC website. What is the company working on? What are the company's projections and goals? Look up the company's website. What do they want their customers to know about them? Research their competitors. What makes them better than the competition? Answers to these questions give you topics of conversation that your interviewer will want to discuss with you. So, ask how that project on their company website is progressing. Ask them how they think their college football team will do this year. Tell them how terrible their competitor's ad campaign looks. No matter what topics you choose, find a way to carry on a conversation further than, "How are you doing? Good. Good." Most interviews will be scheduled for about 30 minutes to an hour. So, if you are able to comfortably carry on the small talk for ten minutes, as much as one-third of your interview will be spent becoming friends with your interviewer. That personal connection will put the interviewer in your corner, and they will actually be pulling for you throughout the interview.

There are, however, a couple of cautions when it comes to small talk. The first is, never assume that you and your interviewer are equals. Everything you say and ask should reflect professionalism and a respect for your interviewer. You are looking to be part of a company where you have yet to earn respect or pay your dues. Make sure that your words and mannerisms reflect that. The second caution is don't be "creepy." When researching your interviewer, you are trying to find safe topics of conversation to casually bring up. However, you will seem like a stalker if you tell your interviewer, "I saw your family on Facebook. You have adorable children." Don't be that person. That person doesn't get hired; that person gets a restraining order.

- Dress The Part

The next topic we will discuss is what to wear for your interview. Now we will not dive into whether you should use a half Windsor or full Windsor knot on your tie or if your shirt should have a front pocket. Those types of details could fill their own book, and I highly recommend you find and skim it before selecting your wardrobe. Instead, let's look at why what your wear matters and what it tells your interviewer about you, the person.

How you are dressed should transmit two very important messages: I will learn and follow the rules, and I care about impressing you. Not only are these the two messages your clothing should tell your interviewer, but they are the **ONLY** two messages that your clothing should convey to your interviewer. This is not the time to express to everyone that you are a beautiful and unique snowflake with a phenomenally innovative and risk-taking style. When you try to standout with something as trivial as the clothing you choose to wear, you are telling the interviewer that you believe your wants and desires are more important or valuable than those of the organization. You are telling them that you will not conform to their culture, and that you push back on any direction given to you, no matter how meaningless.

Take for example men's clothing in a corporate or office environment. For the interview you should wear a dark blue or black suit, a white shirt, a tie with a simple pattern (preferably fewer than three colors), black socks (no pattern), and brown or black dress shoes that match your belt. That's it. If you are thinking to yourself, "What about..." just stop there. The answer is "No." That "fun" tie or those colorful socks tell your interviewer that you are not taking the job opportunity seriously. Even something as benign as a tan suit gives your interviewer the subconscious message that either you haven't done this before or you didn't take the time to learn the rules.

Selecting the correct attire tells your future employers that you will learn and follow the corporate code. You don't have to buy $3,000 suits or handcrafted Italian leather loafers. Whatever you do wear must be clean, pressed, and polished. Unless you are interviewing in the fashion industry, no one knows the difference between Armani and Men's Warehouse, but everyone knows a wrinkled shirt means "I don't care." The same holds true for unpolished shoes and a five o'clock shadow.

For women's clothing there is more leeway, but the message remains the same. You need to look professional, not special. If you are wearing clothing to an interview that you would also wear for a non-work reason, you are wrong.

- You Got to Want It

It is critical to show genuine enthusiasm for the job you seek. To put it simply, if the interviewer doesn't think you want to be there she will not want you to be there either. Think about the last infomercial you saw on television. Have you ever seen anyone that excited about a blender? Are red wine stains really the bane of anyone's existence? Has anyone ever been that pumped about a new towel? Probably not, but those commercials are undeniably effective. The reason they are so effective is that enthusiasm is contagious. By the same token, a lack of enthusiasm can sap excitement in others. The last thing your interviewer is looking to do is to add an energy drain to their organization.

There are several ways to demonstrate enthusiasm for the job you are seeking, and your interviewer will be on the lookout for all of them. Some are obvious. For example, showing up to the interview 10 minutes early shows eagerness and commitment. Arriving five minutes late means you don't value the interviewer's time and this session doesn't mean that much to you. There are other signs that are a little more subtle.

While researching this book, I spoke with a recruiter who shared with me a prime example of the need to be enthusiastic. He told the story of one candidate who went on a tour of the company as part of the interview process. The interviewer shared that although their conversations went well, they would not be offering the candidate a job. When asked why, the interviewer said that the candidate walked too slowly and did not keep up on the tour. The interviewer believed that the candidate would not be able to keep up with the demands and speed of the job.

You may think this is unbelievable. How can someone discount an otherwise qualified candidate simply because of his walking pace? That, however, was not what was being evaluated. The recruiter was using his pace as a proxy for his passion for the job. Don't think that any detail is too small to be used to your benefit. Always show excitement for the opportunity as well as a strong desire to be a part of the team.

- It's Not a Trick Question

There is one answer in the interview process that is completely unacceptable and will ruin your chances of being hired. That answer is "I don't know." Never say, "I don't know," and leave it at that. In most cases this is the only wrong answer to any question posed. Even if you don't know the answer to the question, tell your interviewer how you would find the answer or how you would solve the problem of not knowing. Remember, it's not a trick question. Trick questions have right and wrong answers. This is a process question, and process questions don't have right and wrong answers. They have right and wrong processes.

Many interviewers will try to elicit this response from you in numerous different ways. They will ask you seemingly ridiculous questions such as "How many basketballs can fit in a Nissan Sentra?" Or "How many cell phones are there in the state of Texas?" These questions seem ridiculous because it is obvious that questioners don't care about the right answer. They do, however, care about how you think, and how you problem-solve.

Let's look at the "How many basketballs fit in a Nissan Sentra?" Here is an example of how to answer:

"Well the average basketball is around 1ft in diameter. Since they don't stack perfectly, they probably take up about 1 cubic foot of space each if you fit them into a container. The inside of a Sentra is around 4 feet from the floor to the roof and around 6 feet from the front to the back. It is also about 5 feet across. So that gives us 4*6*5ft or 120 cubic feet of space. Let's say that about 1/2 of that space is taken up by the seats, dashboard, and windshield. Therefore, there is about 60 cubic feet for the basketballs. I would estimate that you could fit 60 basketballs in a Nissan Sentra."

A couple of things should jump out at you. First, I didn't just say 60 basketballs. That would make me sound like Rainman. The interviewer would assume I am just making up an answer or I'm a weirdo who stacks sports equipment in sedans in my spare time. Also, all my assumptions were specific and reasonable, but they made the math very easy. This is the key to these questions. Can you make reasonable assumptions, and can you think critically based on these assumptions? It doesn't do you any good to say that the diameter of a basketball is 9.51 inches and the width of a Nissan Sentra is 5.77 ft and then waste 20 minutes with your phone's calculator.

If you demonstrate the ability to think critically and not be thrown for a loop at a curveball question, you will have passed the test the question posed. The best way to work through these questions is to briefly explain your assumptions and show your work on some scratch paper. It doesn't matter if you are correct or not. It matters if you can work under pressure.

- The Devil is in the Details

Think about the last time you met someone new. How long did it take for you to determine if you liked them? How long did it take to realize that you wouldn't get along? Odds are it was a pretty quick determination. In fact, it was probably something rather minute that determined that for you. Most people make these determinations very quickly, often just by looking at a person. This is a process known as thin slicing. This process of thin slicing is detailed expertly in Malcom Gladwell's book *Blink*. (If you haven't read that yet, I highly recommend it). In this process people make decision by extrapolating information from small cues.

Have you ever looked at a person's haircut and thought, "We probably differ politically?" Have you ever seen a person's glasses and thought, "I bet she is smart," or "He must be an artist." Has someone's phone ever gone off in an important meeting? What did you think about them? People do this all the time, and it is mostly done subconsciously. Understand that your interviewer is doing the same thing. They are subconsciously evaluating you on seemingly minor details.

So how do we know we are sending the right messages? How do we know interviewers will like us? The answer is simple – mirror them. People like themselves and they like people who are similar to them. Try to match your interviewers' mannerisms. If they speak quickly pick up the pace of your own conversation. If they speak with their hands use some gestures when you answer as well. If they lean in, you should do the same. The key is to be subtle. You are not a mime matching every movement. This is more about matching tone and expression.

Another detail to be aware of is posture. Maintain your posture throughout the interview. Standing tall and sitting up straight shows a confidence and attention to detail. Pay attention to this in others. What do you think about someone who is slouching back in their chair? What about someone who is hunched over their phone while standing? Your interviewer is making similar judgments about you.

- Q&A

At the end of the interview your interviewer will most likely ask if you have any questions for them. That does not mean that the evaluation is over. Your interviewer is absolutely evaluating you based on the questions you will ask them. Ensure that the questions you are asking tell them something positive about yourself.

Many people will make the mistake of thinking that this is an opportunity for them to evaluate the position or company they are applying for. This is absolutely not the time to do this. Remember, you do not have an offer yet, and until you do, every part of the process is about making the company want you. For example, people will ask about things like time off and benefits. Really? You haven't worked one day at the company and you are already concerned about time off or the dental plan. This screams that you only view this job as a paycheck and that you will not be dedicated to this position. This goes for everything from expected travel to 401k plans. You don't have an offer yet, so now is not the time to evaluate one. Don't raise any concerns about yourself or why you may not be a fit for the position until the company has made the decision that it wants you.

Another mistake people often make at this point of the interview is not having any questions for the interviewer. That basically tells the interviewer that you are not curious about the role or how to succeed in it. Not having questions ready means that you either didn't research the role or you don't care enough about it to ask. Either way it is a big red flag in your interviewer's mind.

So what questions should you ask? Put yourself in the interviewer's shoes. What would you want a potential candidate to be curious about? What if they asked, "You have a lot of experience in this company. What have you seen that separates the people who are exceptional at this role from those who are average?" What if you asked, "What should I be doing right now to prepare myself to hit the ground running when I start with you?" How about, "What books would you recommend to prepare me for this role?" Always ask questions with answers the interview wants to give you. This shows that your only concern is being successful and making their lives easier.

Ask questions that give you an opportunity to show off your preparation. For example, ask things like, "I was reading up on your competitor and they are about to launch product X. How are we preparing to counter that?" Ask questions that allow them to brag about their company such as, "Customer's in this industry seem to value convenience very highly. How does this company separate themselves from the competition in this area?" You could also ask, "I have been doing a lot of research about this company and I think we would be a great fit. What about this company are you most proud of?"

You should have several of these questions ready to go. Ask a few to show that you are genuinely interested in this specific company, and when they answer tie their answer into why that makes you want to work there even more.

- Close, Close, Close

If you remember nothing else from this book, remember this: **You have to close**. The close is when you ask for the job, and the interviewer gives you a "yes" or a "no." If you don't close you will not get the job. Period. You must put your interviewer on the spot. I have talked to several people who have not hired candidates for the sole reason that they didn't close in the interview. This cannot be stressed enough. You must close them.

I know what you are thinking. People don't like being put on the spot. What if I put them on the spot and they say, "No?" What if they have other candidates still to interview? What if there are other people at the company who I still need to interview with?

Let's start with the first point: people don't like being put on the spot. This is true, but this exactly why you should do it. The truth is people don't like having to say "No" to people. No one cares about being put on the spot to give good news. You need to use this to your advantage. Since no one wants to deliver bad news face to face, they are more likely to say yes or move you forward in the process and let someone else make the decision.

What if they say no? If you read the situation properly throughout this process you will know before asking what their answer will be. However, to mitigate the risk of their saying "No" as well as to give you options if they do, you need to focus on how you ask. Memorize this closing, and use it in your next interview:

"Mr. Interviewer, from what we discussed today I know I can bring a lot of value to your organization and I think I would be a perfect fit on your team. Is there anything we discussed that I can clarify that would prevent you from moving me forward in this process?"

With this close you have given yourself an out while at the same time putting the onus on the interviewer to tell you that you have their approval. If the interviewer says that there is something that would prevent your moving forward, you have already stated an intent to "clarify" that issue. With your clarification, you will have the opportunity to overcome their objection. Once you address their concern, ask again "Is there anything else that would prevent us from taking the next steps?" This expresses that you have moved past that issue and are ready to proceed.

Once you get your interviewer to confirm that there is nothing else that would prevent them from moving you forward in the process, you are not done. Leaving the conversation with agreement to move forward is the rookie move and not a true close. A true close defines the next step and puts a deadline on it. When your interviewer says there is nothing else to discuss that would prevent your advancing to the next phase, ask them what that next step is and when it will be completed. Remember, if a time is not established for the next interaction before leaving, it may never take place.

What if they have other candidates to interview? This is another reason you need to close. What you are doing is asking them to choose between you, the person who just impressed them in an interview, and someone else who is an unknown commodity. At this point in time you have the advantage over every other candidate they have yet to meet. This is the perfect time to ask for their approval to move forward, because it eliminates the "I like them, but I like this other person better" objection. Also, if there are more people to interview, asking to be moved forward in the process will ensure your spot on the short list of candidates who will receive a second interview. Going for the close can only help you, and ignoring the opportunity will only hurt.

What if I need to interview with other people in the company? Perfect. Once you close the person you are interviewing with ask them for a recommendation with the next person you are going to meet. This could be the next step you are closing them on. Getting your interviewer to recommend you to the next person you meet with will not only set you up for success in the next interview, but also forces the original interviewer to defend you when decision-makers compare notes. The bottom line is there is no reason not to ask your interviewer to either move you forward in the process or help in getting you the position.

- Thank you

Once you leave the interview, you are not done. Just as your mother told you that you had to write thank you notes for your birthday gifts, you need to write thank you notes to your interviewer. This is not a "nice to do" option. It is a requirement of the interview process. Everyone you meet with should get a thank you note. These notes should be personalized and reference something that was brought up in your conversation. Mail your thank-you notes. Email is a last resort, as it shows that you are only willing to do the bare minimum. An actual letter is memorable. It means that you took some time and effort. That is the kind of person that your interviewer is looking for. Neglecting this step translates as ungrateful, and ungrateful is unacceptable. An email translates to lazy. Don't do all the work of preparation, research, and rehearsal for the interview just to be seen as cutting corners once you walk out of the office.

Chapter 8

Conclusion

While in the military, I had the pleasure to serve under one of the best leaders I have ever come in contact with. There was one piece of guidance Lt. Col. O'Neal gave me that has always stood out in my mind. While addressing his junior officers he said, "Confidence comes from competence." On the surface this may seem like a simple platitude, but when you analyze this statement it is actually an extremely powerful key to success in any endeavor.

Confidence is often the deciding factor in any interview you will ever participate in, no matter the setting. Think about any date you have ever been on. These are obviously much more casual than a typical job interview, but they are interviews nonetheless. Just like a job interview, both people are spending time together to determine if the other person is someone they want to enter into a relationship with. Both parties are attempting to display the best version of themselves while trying to understand the other person. No matter what magazine article or blog you read or what relationship guru you listen to, they all echo the same thing. Be yourself and be confident. Confidence is often rated as the most attractive attribute a person can have. It doesn't matter if you are trying to get a second date or a second interview, confidence is the key to success.

Now, I know what you are probably thinking. "That's great and all, but how do I magically exude confidence in such an important and nerve-racking experience as a job interview?" The answer lies in Lt. Col. O'Neal's guidance to his team. Confidence comes from competence. The only way to gain competence is through preparation.

This book reveals the secret language of the interview. You now know what information your interviewer is really seeking to uncover with the questions they ask. In addition, you have learned how to craft your response to give them exactly that information in a way that will resonate. Now all that is left to do is practice. First, practice how to identify the category of question being asked. How many different ways can you think of that your interviewer might ask you to tell them about a great accomplishment? How many ways could they ask you to tell them about your weaknesses? Search online for common interview questions and determine what category they fall into. Once you are **confident** in your ability to identify the information they are after, start working on crafting your response to each one.

When you begin working on your responses, start by coming up with three to five stories, examples, or experiences you can share for each question. Dissect each one. What does that story tell about you? How does the message change as you tweak each response? Continue to focus each answer until you are **confident** in the exact message your interviewer will take away from your responses. Practice saying each response until if flows off your tongue naturally, as if you were conversing with an old friend.

Finally, practice your close. This is where you must display confidence. Keep repeating your close until it feels completely comfortable. It should come off as just another question in your interviewer. If you sound confident in asking for the job, your interviewer will feel confident in offering it to you. If, however, you waver and act unsure, your interviewer will also feel hesitant in accepting you.

The final piece of advice I will share with you is something that one of my coworkers gave me before I was to go on an interview for a promotion within the company. He told me, "Go take what's yours." You have exhaustively prepared for this interview. You know you are a great fit and the best candidate the company will interview. This job is already yours. Now, go take what's yours.

www.ingramcontent.com/pod-product-compliance
Lightning Source LLC
Chambersburg PA
CBHW070050210526
45170CB00012B/638